PENGUINS

Scientific Consultant:
Paul Sweet
American Museum of Natural History

Photo credits:

Tom & Pat Leeson — Front cover; Pages 7-8, 13, 18
Art Wolfe — Front cover; Pages 8-9, 14, 18, 22, 24-25, 28
Francois Gohier — Pages 9, 11, 13, 15-16, 19, 23, 26
Tom Vezo/Wildlife Collection — End Pages; Pages 7-9, 15, 17
H. Rappel/Wildlife Collection — Pages 6, 12
Chris Huss/Wildlife Collection — Pages 13, 16
Stefan Lundgren/Wildlife Collection — Pages 15, 21, 26
Dean Lee/Wildlife Collection — Pages 18-19, 27
Dennis Frieborn/Wildlife Collection — Pages 20, 25
Nora & Rick Bowers/Wildlife Collection — Page 28
Johnny Johnson/DRK — Pages 6-7, 9-11, 14-15, 17, 19-20, 23-24, 27
Norbert Wu/DRK — Page 6
Tom Brakefield/DRK — Page 7
John Eastcott/DRK — Page 8
M.P. Kahl/DRK — Pages 9-10
Ford Kristo (Australia)/DRK — Page 11
Wayne Lynch/DRK — Pages 12-13, 24
Sue Matthews/DRK — Page 14
Leonard Lee Rue III/DRK — Page 16
Lynn M. Stone/DRK — Page 19
Annie Griffiths/DRK — Page 20
Barbara Gerlach/DRK — Page 21
Kim Heacox/DRK — Page 24
Barbara Cushman Rowell/DRK — Page 25
Peter Pickford/DRK — Page 29
Kjell B. Sandved/Visuals Unlimited — Pages 8, 10, 17-18, 22, 26
John Gerlach/Visuals Unlimited — Pages 11, 21
N. Pecnik/Visuals Unlimited — Page 20
Brian Rogers/Visuals Unlimited — Page 21
Courtesy Dept. Library Services/American Museum of Natural History
    Neg. No. 314878/Photo. Julius Kirschner — Page 12
Wildlife Conservation Society — Page 16
Wide World Photos, Inc. — Pages 28-29

EYES ON NATURE™

PENGUINS

Written by
Jane P. Resnick

kidsbooks®
Incorporated

WHAT A BIRD!

You may know them by their waddle and their black and white feathers. But penguins are so much more! All these tough birds are super swimmers. Some live in the bitter cold, as far south as Antarctica, where ice presents another fun way to travel.

OLD BIRD
Penguins are an ancient bird family. Fossils 50 to 60 million years old have been found on the coasts of New Zealand and Australia.

WATER WAYS
Ancestors of penguins were probably able to fly. But today's penguins fly only underwater. Some spend as much as 75 percent of their time in the ocean, where they make very deep dives to find food.

◀ Penguins don't fly, but they can leap!

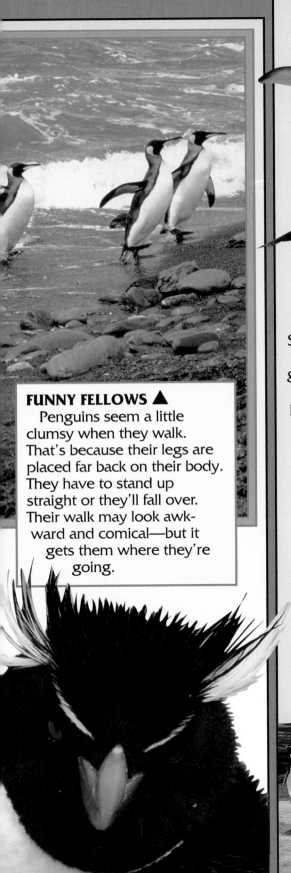

◀PERFECT PENGUIN

Go to the zoo and you'll most likely see Adélie (uh-DAY-lee) Penguins. There are more Adélies than any other kind of penguin in captivity. Adélies are medium-sized—about 10 pounds and 2¹/₂ feet tall. Wearing a "tuxedo," they're everybody's idea of what a penguin looks like. But nature has created different kinds of penguins.

PENGUIN PARTIES

Penguins have very active social lives. Some species gather in huge, noisy groups to find mates and breed. These places, called "rook-eries," are penguin cities, filled with thousands upon thousands of birds.

FUNNY FELLOWS ▲

Penguins seem a little clumsy when they walk. That's because their legs are placed far back on their body. They have to stand up straight or they'll fall over. Their walk may look awk-ward and comical—but it gets them where they're going.

NAME THAT BIRD

Penguins have wonderful names. The King and Emperor are the largest. The Chinstrap is named for its special markings. The Rockhopper's name comes from its fancy footwork (shown below) in bouncing from rock to rock.

◀ The Rockhopper Penguin

SO DIFFERENT!

Will the real penguin please stand up? There are 17 species of penguins, and no two are exactly alike. Some have orange head tufts that look like crazy eyebrows. Some have brushy tails. Some are aggressive. Others are mild-mannered.

An Emperor Penguin and chick

HEAVYWEIGHTS

Three and a half feet and over 60 pounds is a lot of bird. That's the Emperor, the largest of all. The King Penguin is the next heaviest at about 35 pounds. With lovely orange or yellow patches around their ears, and brilliant orange around their neck, the Kings are very handsome birds.

The King Penguin

PINT-SIZED PENGUIN

The shy Little Penguin is so delicate, it has been called the Fairy Penguin. It grows to only a foot and a half, weighs under three pounds, and is the smallest of all penguins.

FEATHERED FRIENDS

The Macaroni Penguin has a "crest" of orange and yellow feathers. It gets its name from a fancy hairstyle that was popular among young men in England during the late 18th and early 19th centuries.

LOUDMOUTH
The Chinstrap is one of the brush-tailed penguins, which have long tails that sweep behind them. The Chinstrap stands a little over two feet tall and has a black stripe across its chin. It also has an ear-splitting call.

DONKEY CALL
A penguin that looks like it's been standing in the mud is the Black-footed Penguin. Its less lovely name is the Jackass Penguin because it makes a loud bray-ing noise like a donkey.

YELLOW-EYED
The Yellow-eyed is the fourth tallest penguin, after the Emperor and King. A bit different from the black-and-white variety of penguins, the Yellow-eyed has a slate-blue back, white undersides, and striking yellow eyes.

JUMPING GENTOO
A white band that goes from eye to eye is the mark of the Gentoo Penguin. This 14-pound bird, sometimes called the Johnny Penguin, runs, jumps, and even slides on its belly on sand.

BOLD LIVING

Penguins live only below the equator. Some come ashore on Antarctica, frigid home of the South Pole. But others do not live in cold places. They are found on the coasts and islands of South America, Africa, Australia, and New Zealand.

Equator

South America

South Atlantic Ocean

Africa

Galápagos Islands

Indian Ocean

Antarctica

South Pacific Ocean

New Zealand

Australia

► These Emperor Penguins enjoy the ease of ice travel in Antarctica.

ICE ISLAND

Antarctica, covered by a sheet of ice nearly a mile thick, is one of the coldest places on Earth. This continent is the breeding ground of the Adélie, Emperor, Chinstrap, and Gentoo penguins. But the Emperor is the only penguin that spends the winter there.

Adélies in a snowstorm.

▲ BIRD-WATCHING

The first time Europeans set eyes on a penguin was when explorer Vasco da Gama sailed down the coast of Africa in 1499. One surprised sailor reported that he saw birds that couldn't fly, and which made a sound like a mule. Almost 500 years later, the Black-footed Penguin is still there, living on the coasts and small islands around the southern tip of Africa.

HOMEBODIES ▼

The coasts of New Zealand, Australia, and some surrounding islands are the homes of Little Penguins. These birds don't migrate like some other penguins. They travel only between their nest and the sea, about a third of a mile. It's a short but risky trip, threatened by the likes of cats, dogs, weasels, and even cars.

HOT AND COLD

Galapagos Penguins make their nests on the Galapagos Islands, off the coast of South America. That's nearly on the equator, a very hot spot! But the ocean there is cold, fed by a current flowing from the icy Antarctic— and filled with the foods that penguins like to eat.

NAMESAKE ▼

Magellanic Penguins have a name from the history books. When Ferdinand Magellan, the Portuguese explorer, led the first expedition around the world in 1519, he sailed around the tip of South America. That's where the Magellanics live, on both the Pacific and Atlantic coasts.

▼ Galapagos Penguins share their home with another ocean-goer— the marine iguana.

WARM BODIES

Penguins are warm-blooded creatures, just like people. Their normal body temperature is 100 to 102°F. Ours is 98.6°F. How do they stay warm in icy waters? Layers of insulation. Under their skin they have fat, known as blubber. Covering the skin are fluffy feathers, called *down,* and a tightly packed layer of outer feathers, which seals in warmth.

CUDDLE HUDDLE ▲

Emperor penguins have the coldest breeding grounds—in Antarctica. They incubate their eggs in extreme weather, standing motionless on the ice. Sometimes one body just doesn't create enough heat. So they form a tight huddle. That's as many as 6,000 penguins squeezing shoulder to shoulder!

◀ BONE BONUS

Normally, birds have light, hollow bones that make flight easier. But penguins have heavy, solid bones that suit their way of life in the water. The weight lets them get their body underwater—where they can use their powerful flippers to swim.

SUPER FEET

There's more to penguins than feathers. Look at their feet. On land, penguins can walk, run, and hop. At sea, they use their webbed feet as rudders for steering.

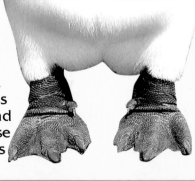

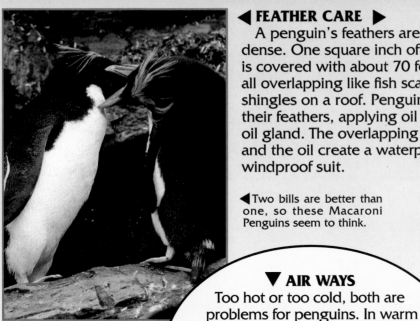

◀ FEATHER CARE ▶

A penguin's feathers are slick and dense. One square inch of penguin is covered with about 70 feathers, all overlapping like fish scales or shingles on a roof. Penguins *preen* their feathers, applying oil from an oil gland. The overlapping feathers and the oil create a waterproof, windproof suit.

◀ Two bills are better than one, so these Macaroni Penguins seem to think.

This ▶ Gentoo gets its feathers ready for the water by preening.

▼ AIR WAYS

Too hot or too cold, both are problems for penguins. In warm places, such as the Galapagos Islands, penguins need to cool off. Feather fluffing is the answer. Penguins can lift their feathers and keep them up, so air can cool their skin. They also stick out their winglike flippers to help heat escape.

MADE TO MOLT ▼

Feathers don't last forever. Most birds replace them by *molting,* shedding old feathers and growing new ones. But penguins need their feathers in the icy sea. They molt all at once, and during that time—as long as a month—they stay out of the water.

COLOR COATED

Color counts when a penguin is trying to keep warm. Black absorbs heat, and white reflects heat. A chilly penguin turns its black back to the sun and absorbs the warmth. A penguin in danger of overheating turns its white chest to the sun to reflect light.

This Galapagos Penguin stretches out its flippers to cool off.

WATER WINGS

A penguin is a bird that "flies" underwater. Unlike other birds, penguins have short stiff paddlelike wings called flippers. Underwater, they propel themselves forward in a flying motion, flapping their wings about two times a second, just as other birds do in the air.

SHAPED TO SWIM ▲

Look at a penguin underwater and think of a submarine or torpedo. With this sleek streamlined body, penguins can slice through water like a seal or dolphin. Their average swimming speed is 15 miles per hour.

▲ Rockhoppers make spectacular leaps.

DEEP DIVERS

No bird can dive like a penguin. A penguin will drop 70 feet just to grab a meal. Penguins are known to stay underwater for up to 18 minutes. Emperor Penguins have been observed 1200 feet below the surface of the water—an amazing and probably rare dive.

These ▶ Adélies are ready to dive in!

14

LEAPING FOR AIR ▼
"Porpoising" is the penguin way of breathing while swimming. Penguins speed up underwater, shoot out above the surface, and breathe. Then they dive back under for another go-around.

◀ UP AND OVER
Going from water onto land is a simple task for penguins. They just waddle out. But when they face steep walls of ice, snow, or rock, they leap. They dive down and then swim up so rapidly that they shoot out of the water—as high as 6 feet—and land safely on their feet.

SPEED SLIDE
To move faster on ice, penguins *toboggan.* They lie belly-down on the ground, push with their feet and flippers, and glide like a person on a sled. This speeds them up from two or three miles an hour walking, to eight miles an hour tobogganing.

SEAFOOD

For penguins, fish is always on the menu. They also eat krill, crustaceans, and squid. Krill are tiny shrimplike animals found in enormous numbers. The world's penguin population eats tons of krill every day. In Antarctica, during mating season when millions of penguins gather, they may eat half of the Antarctic Ocean's available food.

FISHING GEAR ▼

For snapping up a meal, penguins have fishing equipment—a sharp bill with hooks that fit together. Their tongue is equipped with backwards-facing bristles that grab the wiggling prey and thrust it down the throat.

◀ Krill

PICKY PENGUINS

Just like people, penguins have food preferences. The Adélies' favorite is krill. Magellanics go for squid, and Black-footed Penguins want fish and more fish. Of course, where they live, how deep they dive, and what swims by has a lot to do with what each penguin eats.

SALTSHAKER ▼

Surrounded by salt-water, penguins can't get fresh water to drink. So their body "makes" fresh water for them. Penguins have a gland that removes the salt from the water and releases it through grooves in their bill.

▼ MOUTH TO MOUTH

Food for chicks comes straight from a parent's mouth. The adults return with undi-gested food stored in their *crop,* a special pouch in the throat. A chick fits its bill inside the adult's mouth to receive the food. An Emperor par-ent may deliver seven pounds of food at a time to its chick.

BODY STORAGE

An Emperor Penguin's large body is built to store food. During the whole breeding period they eat nothing. It is not until the egg is laid that one parent leaves for the sea to eat. An Emperor male, who goes without food longer than any other penguin—for 15 weeks or more in -40°F weather—loses nearly half his body weight. When he does eat, the Emperor dad may con-sume 30 pounds of food at one time.

17

THE MATING GAME

In the mating season, all penguins head for land. Each species has its own territory, and some are very far from their ocean homes. The Adélies nest in the spring, which begins in October in Antarctica. But the land is still surrounded by sea ice. To reach their rookery, the penguins trudge across the ice—for as much as 60 miles! ▶

◀ CHILLY WINTER

Emperor Penguins start breeding in the winter, which begins in March. There is no sun at that time. The penguins stay on the grim ice for six months, until their chicks are ready to be on their own when summer arrives.

SHOW-OFFS ▶

A male penguin has a walk that gets females to follow him. It's called a "display" or "advertisement walk."

The King Penguin, with his spectacular orange neck markings, is the best on the block. He struts and turns his head from side to side so the female can see just how handsome he is.

LOVE CALL

There is high drama in the rookeries when mating begins. Each male must attract a female, and they do it by "calling." They stand with their back arched, head raised, and wings outstretched, and raise a wild trumpeting cry.

TUNE FOR TWO

All penguin pairs "sing" a duet as part of their display, and it's not just for entertainment. They learn to recognize each other's voice. That's very important because there are thousands of look-alikes in a rookery.

▼ YOU'RE MINE!

When a male and female become a pair, they cement the bond in a "mutual display." The two penguins, depending on the species, may raise their heads, touch necks, vibrate their flippers, or slap each other on the back.

PENGUIN PAIRS

Most penguins stick to the same partner. One theory for this behavior is that most return to their old territory and meet up automatically. But some scientists believe that penguins recognize each other by voice and sight, even after a year.

NEST, SWEET NEST

To build a nest, to find a mate, and to breed—that is the life's work of a penguin. All species are similar in these activities, but they are different, too. Just look at their nests!

▲ GHOSTLY GROUND

On the eastern coast of Argentina, there is an eerie noise that comes from holes in the ground, inspiring legends of ghosts and even devils. The sound comes from penguins—thousands of Magellanics, whose dug-in burrows form huge underground cities.

Black-footed Penguins dig burrows, too, ▶ but will also build nests above ground, using vegetation, feathers, or stones.

A Rockhopper and its egg.

BOUNCING BIRDS

Rockhoppers build nests on steep rocky areas. They get there by jumping. With both feet held together, they bounce 4 to 5 feet from one ledge to another. Macaroni Penguins build their nests on steep, rough ground, too. Sometimes they build on lava flows, rock slopes, and in caves.

▲ Nesting Macaroni mates.

PRECIOUS STONES ▶

Stones are like diamonds to Adélies. Stones are the only material they have to build their nests on Antarctica. Sometimes the right-sized rocks are in short supply. So every Adélie watches its stones, or a neighbor will steal them!

◀ MALE DUTY

As soon as eggs are laid, the female heads for the sea to find food. The male stays with the eggs. By the time the Adélie female returns, the males haven't eaten for about two weeks. Then it's his turn to eat while she stays with the egg.

TAKING TURNS ▶

Gentoos hollow a nest in the ground and line it with grass. Then the male and female take turns keeping the egg warm against their *brood patch,* a featherless area on the belly.

FOOTHOLD

King Penguins have a territory rather than a nest. They incubate an egg standing up, and the spot where they stand is theirs. The sea is close to their colony, so parents eat and return often.

LIVING TOGETHER

Gather thousands of penguins together and what have you got? A rookery. Large rookeries can cover miles. But each pair of penguins gets only about one square yard of space to build a nest. It's crowded and noisy, but it's home.

▼ VOICES CARRY

Penguins get along in these huge throngs by "calling"—a cross between trumpets blaring and donkeys braying. Each species has its own unique call. Each penguin has its own particular sound. And they locate one another by voice. Shouting, they let each other know to "watch out" or "stay clear!"

In a rookery, it gets really crowded!

◄ King Penguins communicating.

◀ BODY LANGUAGE

Penguins communicate by gesture as well as by voice. They bump, paddle, and peck. They stare, bow, and crouch. Through sound and movement, they let others know their situation. They are male or female. They need a mate or don't. They want a nest or have one. They like each other or not.

SAFE CIRCLE ▼

For almost all animals, there is safety in numbers, especially when it comes to the young. When chicks are strong enough, both parents head for the sea. The chicks group together in a *creche,* or nursery, where they're less likely to be attacked by predators.

▼ Emperor chicks have to huddle to keep warm.

MA! IT'S ME! ▶

Ever get lost? Imagine looking for your parents among millions of others! But in the penguin world, chicks and parents recognize each other's calls and always find one another. Even while the chick is breaking out of its egg, it is calling so its parent will get to know its voice.

23

CHICK TIME

Male and female penguins really work together when it's time to build a nest, lay eggs, and raise chicks. The survival of their baby depends on their cooperation. It's a tough job for the chicks, too, just to grow up.

BABIES ON ICE ▼

Being born in Antarctica is like beginning life in a freezer. When they hatch, chicks are helpless and cold. They have soft down feathers instead of the sleek, waterproof coats of their parents. The Emperor chick must stand on a parent's feet, not touching the ice for the first two months of its life, or it will freeze.

▼ Emperor chick

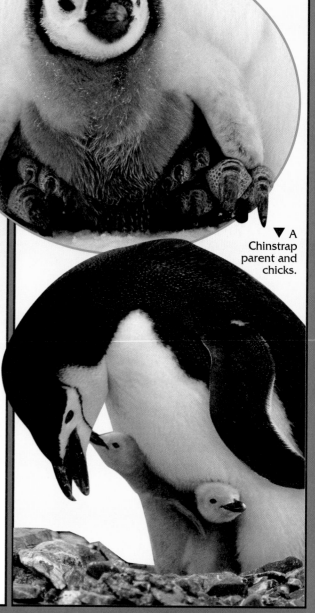

▼ A Chinstrap parent and chicks.

ONE CHICK, OR TWO?

Penguins may lay two eggs, but sometimes only one survives. The Chinstrap usually lays two same-sized eggs. The eggs hatch on the same day, and the chicks are treated equally. But Gentoos lay two different-sized eggs, the larger one first. The smaller chick may not survive if there's not enough food for both.

◀ This newly hatched Gentoo chick enjoys a foot seat.

◄NEST REST

Chicks hatched in a nest will stay there for awhile. It is their period of *brooding,* a time when their parents still keep them warm and protected. A Rockhopper chick stays around its nest for about three weeks, but by ten weeks it has gone to sea.

◄ King Penguin chicks form a creche after about three weeks, when they have a layer of thick brown down.

CHICK CLUB

Some chicks don't hang out in their nest until they're old enough to leave. They form a creche instead. When parents return from gathering food, the chicks break from their group and chase their parents down. Then the parents feed them.

TO BE A BIG BIRD

When chicks grow their adult feathers and are ready to go to sea, they are said to be *fledging.* King chicks stay in their creche for about nine months before they molt and leave. Afterward, they no longer depend on their parents.

A molting King Penguin chick.

25

PREYING ON PENGUINS

Penguins fall prey to many different predators, especially to leopard seals. The seals hide below the ice and wait for the penguins to jump into the sea. One leopard seal can eat 15 Adélie penguins in one day.

◀ This seal is pursuing some Gentoo Penguins.

▼ Penguins will jump over cracks in the ice to avoid leopard seals.

SAFETY SUIT

A black-and-white swimsuit means safety for a penguin. If a predator is below, looking up, it may not see the penguin's white underside because it would blend in with the light of the sky. If the enemy is above, looking down, it cannot see the penguin's black back against the ocean's dark depths.

FOOD THIEF

Sheathbills are pigeonlike birds in the Antarctic that attack when parents feed their chicks. The sheathbill alarms the penguins, causing the food to fall to the ground. The thief then grabs the prize, flies home, and feeds its own chicks.

◀ A leopard seal.

A penguin tries to protect its ▶ egg from a sheathbill, which eats penguin eggs as well as penguin food.

26

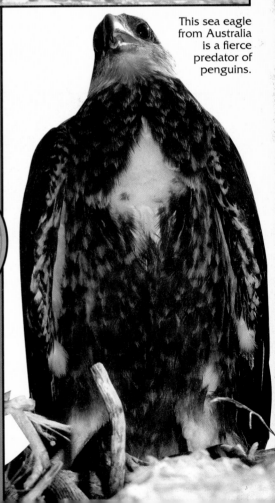

This sea eagle from Australia is a fierce predator of penguins.

▲ BODY SNATCHER

In the Antarctic, skuas swoop down and feed on penguin chicks. To avoid adult penguins, who could defend a chick, the skua may push and roll the little bird away from the rookery where it can more easily be attacked.

Penguins have to watch out for this sneaky blue-tongued lizard.

HAZARDS AT HOME

The penguin enemy list is greater on land than at sea. In Australia, penguins have to watch out for birds of prey, tiger snakes, lizards, foxes, cats, and rats.

27

PENGUINS AND PEOPLE

Penguins and people are not always a good mix. Although people enjoy these amazing water birds, penguins reap few benefits from people. For one thing, people and penguins eat some of the same foods. The penguin population requires millions of fish to survive. The more fish people take from the sea, the fewer there are for penguins.

Taking a group of penguins for a walk, this zookeeper is on good terms with his birds.

LAMP OIL

At one time penguin fat was used as a source for lamp oil. On the Macquarie Islands of New Zealand, 150,000 Royal Penguins are said to have been killed every year between 1894 and 1914 just to make oil.

◀ Royal Penguins

TOURIST TROUBLE ▼

People who visit penguins in their natural habitat sometimes interrupt the care of eggs and the feeding of chicks, which can be a real hazard in the penguin world.

FERTILE GROUND
Guano, the droppings of seabirds, is valuable to people and penguins. People use it for fertilizer. Black-footed Penguins in Africa use it for nesting material. Because people have taken so much of the guano, penguins have lost breeding ground.

Oil-soaked penguins await a bath.

DEADLY SPILLS
Oil spills are a great danger to penguins. Feathers that are soaked and clogged with oil cannot protect the birds from the cold. If the penguins try to clean off the oil, they can be poisoned. At that point, conservationists often rush to the penguins' rescue and try to save as many as they can.

These penguins have been cleansed of oil and are now happily heading home.

PROTECTION
Certain penguin species are considered endangered, but now penguins are protected by law. The effort to safeguard them began in the early 1900s. In 1959, twelve nations signed the Antarctic Treaty to save the area and its animals from further destruction.

10